Jungle Jenny

Eve Cowen

A BESTELLERS BOOK

JOHN MURRAY
London

Series director: Robert G. Bander
Designer: Richard Kharibian
Cover designer and illustrator: Mary Burkhardt
Copyright © 1979 by Fearon Pitman Publishers, Inc. This edition
© 1979 by John Murray (Publishers) Ltd.

Printed in the USA
ISBN–0–7195–3694–4

CONTENTS

CHAPTER **1**

A NEW LIFE

"Thanks so much," Jenny Parker said. "I was really in a jam!" She got her bag out of the car.

The soldier looked at her. Then he gave her a big smile. Jenny smiled too. He doesn't understand one word I've said, she thought.

It had been like that all the way from the airport. She spoke English. He spoke Portuguese. But they had been able to talk with their hands and smiles, and the miles to Bodine Ranch went by fast.

The soldier started the engine and waved goodbye.

"Obrigada," Jenny called. At least she knew one Portuguese word—the one for thank you. "Obrigada!"

Jenny picked up her bag and headed towards the house. What a simple little place, she thought. It was not at all what she had thought she would see. But then everything about the country was so different. Beautiful, but strange. Jenny had never been outside the United States before. She had to keep telling herself, over and over, that Brazil would not be like home.

She looked around. There were so many new things all at once, she thought. The green of the jungle, close around the house. The insects buzzing everywhere. And the humidity was like a wet blanket all around her.

And where was Cliff? Where in the world was Cliff Bodine?

An old woman came out of the house as Jenny walked up the steps. She began speaking to Jenny at once in Portuguese.

"I'm sorry, I don't speak Portuguese," Jenny said. "I speak English."

The old woman looked at her.

"Senhor Bodine?" Jenny asked. "Where is Senhor Bodine?"

The woman gave her a smile. "Senhor Bodine!" She shook her head. "Away. Gone." She opened the door and said, "Come in. Come."

Jenny took her bag and followed the woman into the house. It was dark inside, but still hot.

Jenny was wet to the skin from the heat. She would have given anything to cool off.

She stood in the centre of the small room and looked around. It was a home—but that was all. It was the simple home of a pioneer in the jungles of Brazil. And she, Jenny Parker, had come a long way to marry that pioneer. The only trouble was—the pioneer seemed to be missing.

"Did Senhor Bodine tell you where he was going?" Jenny asked.

The old woman reached out and took Jenny's hand. Then she pointed to herself. "Dora," she said.

Jenny smiled and pressed Dora's hand. "Well, hello," she said. "I'm Jenny. Jenny Parker. Did Senhor Bodine tell you that I was coming to visit him?"

"Senhor Bodine away," Dora said. "Upriver. Natives." She rolled her eyes. "Big trouble."

Jenny looked at Dora for a few seconds. A nice woman, she thought. But how can I make her understand?

Jenny tried again, speaking slowly. "Dora, didn't Senhor Bodine tell you about me?"

Dora shook her head. "Away. Upriver."

Jenny gave up. Cliff's upriver, she thought. And *I'm* starting to feel lost at sea.

Dora picked up Jenny's bag. "Come, rest," she said. She showed Jenny a small, neat bedroom. "Rest." She smiled and left the room, closing the door behind her.

Does she even know who I am? Jenny thought to herself. Does she think I just decided to drop in?

Then she answered herself out loud. "No, she wasn't expecting me."

Jenny was tired. She wasn't thinking well. She knew a good swim would feel wonderful. But Dora had told her to rest.

I guess I'll rest, Jenny thought. I need to think out what I'm going to do. She looked around the room. All the furniture looked as if it was made by hand.

"This is nice," she said, touching a small chair by the bed. "Cliff told me about the native art. But I didn't expect the handmade furniture."

Then Dora's words came back to her. Natives! Trouble! Upriver! What kind of trouble? She went to the door and looked out. Dora was not in sight.

Suddenly Jenny felt afraid. *Trouble. Upriver*. She went to the window and looked out again. It was dark and she couldn't see very far. The trees seemed to have closed in around the house. What was out there in the jungle?

This hasn't been my day, she thought. Everything had gone wrong from the start. From the minute the plane had landed at Manaus. Cliff had not been there to meet her. After that, nothing was right.

She had waited for hours. There was no

message. She had asked at the airport office. They had looked but said there was no message for anyone.

Finally, a soldier had heard her say the words "Bodine Ranch." Yes, he would take her there. He was going that way. And he got into his car and drove her many miles—just like that.

Cliff had told her Brazil was a friendly country. He was right. Friendly and strange and beautiful. And he had wanted her there to share it all.

"It's real pioneer country, up the Amazon in Manaus," he had said. His eyes had had a happy shine.

They were in Boston then, in her apartment near the Charles River. Cliff was quiet, and different from anyone Jenny had met before.

"You'll love Brazil, Jenny," he had said. "I know you will." He had taken her hand in his.

"Cliff—what you're asking me to do—I don't know. My whole world is here in Boston. I've never wanted to leave it. I love you, but my roots are here in the city."

"You can put down new roots in Brazil," he had said with a smile. "Better roots."

She had pressed her free hand against his cheek. "I have to be sure that we're right for each other before I give up my job and my home," she had told him. "There are so many interesting things to do in Boston, too. And maybe I'm not right for the jungle."

Cliff had leaned forward. "We *are* right for each other, Jenny. And the jungle will welcome you with open arms. The jungle needs strong people—like you and me. You'll have *lots* to do there. Different things, but books and music, too. And fairly new films in Manaus!"

She had laughed and said, "I really don't know why I've never wanted to leave the United States. I'm just funny that way. Most of my friends have travelled all over the world. But not me."

"But we're in love, Jenny," he had said. "Love can change people."

She had wondered. She knew when Cliff returned to Brazil she might never see him again. Could she change?

"We'll be married down there," he had said. "But first I want you to see the country for yourself. I won't hold you to anything. If you don't like it, you can take the next plane back."

"You make it all sound as if it's just around the corner," Jenny had said.

"But it is," Cliff had told her. "You'll fly to Rio. In Rio there's a plane to Manaus. It's as simple as that. I'll be at the airport in Manaus waiting for you. It's an easy trip."

"I guess so," Jenny had said.

"Then not another word about it tonight," Cliff had said. "I'll be in Boston for one more week. You'll have all that time to think it over."

Jenny had thought so, too. A whole week was enough time.

But it was not to happen. The very next day Cliff was on the telephone. "I just heard from Brazil. It's my father. He's sick, and I have to fly back at once."

And he was gone before Jenny had a chance to tell him. She wanted Cliff to know that she had made up her mind. She would go anywhere to be with him.

That was over a month ago. Soon after, he wrote to her that his father had died, but that was all he told her. It was just a short, sad note. Right away she wrote back to Cliff that she was coming to Brazil. He had not answered. But mail from that part of Brazil was always slow.

And now Jenny was at Bodine Ranch. She wondered if Cliff knew she was there. And suppose Cliff hadn't meant what he had said?

Perhaps he had never seen her letter. What if it had been lost in the mail?

Jenny stood at the window, looking out into the dark. Suddenly she heard a sound behind her. She turned. There was a flicker of light under her door. Someone was standing out there. She stood very still, afraid to move, afraid to turn.

Her heart was beating fast. She waited, trying to keep control. Then she walked to the door. It had no lock. She pressed her hands against the door.

"Who are you?" Jenny whispered at the door. "What do you want?"

CHAPTER **2**

ON THE RUN

Jenny asked the question again. "Who are you? What do you want?" But the only answer she got was the beating of her heart.

She waited. Someone stood outside the door, waiting, not moving.

"I know you're there," said Jenny, almost afraid to breathe.

All at once, the door opened, and the room was filled with light. For a second, Jenny could see nothing but light. Then she caught her breath. Standing before Jenny, holding a shining oil lamp, was a young woman.

And there was something else, too. The woman was going to have a baby.

Jenny took a deep breath. "You know, you frightened me," she said. "Why didn't you say something when I talked to you?"

The young woman stared at Jenny but didn't say a word.

"Oh dear," said Jenny. "You don't speak English either." Suddenly the young woman spoke.

"Maria," she said, but that was all.

"Maria," said Jenny. "That's a pretty name. I'm Jenny Parker. Did Cliff tell you about me?"

Maria only looked at her without answering.

Jenny tried again. "Can you tell me how long Senhor Bodine will be gone?"

"Senhor Bodine," said Maria, with a wide smile.

Oh, thought Jenny, I'll never get through to her. "Where is your husband?" she asked in a loud voice. Then, more softly, she said, "Husband? Where is he?" Maybe *he* speaks English, Jenny thought.

Maria stopped smiling. For a second, Jenny thought she had said something wrong.

"Senhor Bodine away," Maria said.

Jenny gasped. She looked hard at the young woman called Maria. A wife. Cliff Bodine had a wife. When he had told Jenny he loved her, he was already married.

All her doubts about leaving Boston came back to her now. He had played games with her that night in Boston. And all the while his wife in Brazil was going to have a baby.

Her heart was beating fast. "No," she said, "no, it can't be!"

She ran out of the room. She had to get away. She had to leave Bodine Ranch before Cliff came back.

Married! He knew I was coming to Brazil. Why didn't he try to stop me? She wondered as she looked for Dora. Was it because he never thought I would do it?

"Dora," she called. "The telephone. Where is it? I must call the airport."

"Telephone?" Dora looked at her in a funny way. She stood in the door and held out her upturned hands.

"Oh no," Jenny said. "No telephone!" This is real pioneer country, she thought. No lights, no telephone. No place for me.

She stayed still for a second. She didn't know what to do. Dora stood in the door, staring at her.

"Dora, I must get to Manaus right away," Jenny said. "Airport. Do you understand?"

"Manaus," Dora said. "Airport."

"I need a car to get to the airport in Manaus," said Jenny, speaking slowly.

"Sim, car," said Dora. She nodded her head up and down.

"Car. Car to Manaus," Jenny said. Then she thought: Pull yourself together, Jenny. If that car is around here, it's up to you to find it. She ran out of the house into the night.

The moon was up now, and bright, but the jungle still looked black and frightening. The sounds of the night screamed at her—monkeys, strange animals, birds, insects. They all seemed to cry to her to go back—back to Boston.

An insect bit her. More came at her. She ran towards the back of the house, waving them off. The moonlight picked out a second building. An old car stood in front of it.

"That's it," said Jenny. "My ride to Manaus." The car door was open. She checked inside. Everything looked in good shape. She couldn't tell if the car had any petrol. And, of course, there was no key.

Now to find the key. Well, *that* will not be easy, she thought.

Jenny found both Dora and Maria in the kitchen. She couldn't look at Maria. It hurt too much.

"I have to use the car," she told Dora. "Do you know where the key is?" Dora gave her a blank look.

"Never mind," said Jenny. "I'll find it."

Jenny checked and found only two bedrooms in the house. She walked into Cliff's room and remembered something. It was Maria's room too. There was a desk in the corner. She saw the car key at once. It was in a dish on top of the desk. She took it and ran out of the room.

"I hope they don't try to stop me," she said to herself. "I'm going to take the car."

She got her bag and stopped at the kitchen door on the way out. "Tell Senhor Bodine I'll leave the car at the airport in Manaus." Maria and Dora did not seem to understand.

She left the house and threw her bag into the car. The engine started with no trouble. She checked to see how much petrol the car had. It was half full.

The car was easy to handle. But as she drove past the house she began to cry. "Stop it, Jenny Parker," she told herself. "He's not worth it. Not worth one small tear." But the tears kept coming.

She turned on to the road that had brought her from the airport and set off for Manaus. There were no cars on the road. There were no lights. There was only Jenny Parker, making her way through the strange, dark land.

She had gone 30 miles. The tears were drying slowly. Still there were no signs of life along the road.

All of a sudden the car began to kick. For a minute she was afraid it was out of control. She looked to see how much petrol was left. Empty! The car came to a dead stop.

"Out of petrol," she said. "I don't believe it. It was half full when I started." She tried the engine again. No luck. She got out of the car and looked around. There was no one about.

Then she turned cold with fear. A shape moved towards her. It moved slowly, under the cover of the trees. She could not see what it was—or who it was.

Jenny reached into the car and grabbed her bag. She turned the car lights off. She began to run. Carrying her suitcase, Jenny ran down the road as fast as she could.

She didn't know who was behind her, but she was not going to stop to find out.

CHAPTER **3**

TRAPPED!

Footsteps! Jenny heard them behind her, running along the road. She heard them above the screaming jungle noises that never stopped.

Am I dreaming all this? she wondered. But the sound was there, behind her. She ran on, faster and faster, gasping for breath.

It's just a dream, she told herself. A bad dream. I'll wake up any minute. Or is it the jungle at night? It makes you see things.

Who was behind her? Who was after her? She decided to see. She turned her head. There was a native, his tall body shining in the moonlight. He walked with quick, even steps. He carried something in his hands. A bow? A gun? She couldn't tell.

Oh no! It came to her. If I can see him under this moon, he can see me. He could kill me in a second. And no one would ever know.

Her heart raced. She did not look where she was going. Her foot hit a stone. She tripped and fell. For a second Jenny lay in the road without moving. The native was close to her now.

No, she thought. Not now, not here. My life isn't going to end here on a road in Brazil.

She got up and began running again. She reached a road that turned to the left. She didn't know where it came from or where it went. She rushed on to it, moving under the trees.

Then, suddenly, Jenny found herself looking at a wide river next to the road. The Amazon! She looked for the native. He was not in sight, but she felt he was there, hiding, waiting.

Far up river she saw lights. Manaus! She began to run.

Manaus, she thought. Manaus and the airport and home. The bad dream would be over. She would be safe and would think no more of Cliff Bodine. Not ever. She would forget him. She would forget the love that had passed between them.

The lights were very close now. She could still feel the native behind her. She knew he was still there.

She gasped. It could not be Manaus ahead. The car had not gone more than 30 miles. And Cliff had said it was farther away than that. Where was she?

She passed some wooden houses. They showed no signs of life. There was no one around, not a person she could turn to for help.

Then she saw some lights along the river bank. She saw a large white boat in the water. Its engine was still, but its lights were on. The crew was busy at work.

"Hello," Jenny called from the river bank. "Can anyone help me?"

No one answered her. She looked behind her. There's one way to get away from that native, she thought. Then she climbed on board the boat and went looking for the captain. She stopped the first person she met. "Captain?" He shook his head and pointed to the wheel-house.

Someone was inside. Jenny went to the door and called to him. "Captain?"

The man turned and stared at her. "Sim." He had on a dirty white suit and cap. He had a nasty look on his face.

It was no time to worry about looks. "Can you help me?" Jenny asked. "My car is out of petrol. I must get to Manaus. Is there a petrol station close by?"

"Petrol station?" the captain asked. "Petrol only for boat."

"You speak English," said Jenny, pleased.

"Sim," the captain said. "I speak very good English."

"Look," Jenny said, "let me explain. I ran out of petrol a mile or so back. I must get my car going again. I have to reach Manaus. Do you know anyone who can help me?" She stopped to catch her breath. She felt she had to say everything all at once.

The captain said, "Sim, only petrol for boat."

"Look Captain," Jenny said, trying again. "Manaus, do you understand? Manaus. I must get to Manaus right away. At once. This minute. I must fly on a plane to the United States."

The captain smiled. "OK, OK, United States." He shouted something to his crew in Portuguese. They began to work quickly.

Jenny watched, surprised. She didn't know what was happening. Then the captain went into the wheel-house.

She waited for a while, but the captain did not return. What do I do now? she wondered. She had an idea. The boat might be going to Manaus. Jenny could go with it.

Then she heard it. The engines were turning over. The boat was under way. The shore dropped out of sight. The boat was moving up-river fast.

But no one had told her where they were going.

Suddenly Jenny felt tired. So tired that all she wanted to do was sleep. She looked around. She wanted to sit far away from everyone and everything.

That was when she saw him. The native. He

was sitting on the boat in the dark, still as stone.

"Oh no," she said, "it can't be." He had followed her on board. She turned and ran forward, straight into the captain's arms.

"Oh," he said, laughing, showing ugly yellow teeth. "United States of America."

"Captain, please help me," Jenny said. "He's here. The native. He followed me on board."

The captain still held her. He kept laughing. "Come," he said, pointing below deck. "You come with me."

Jenny felt like a wild animal in a corner. Trapped!

The crew stood around and watched. They did not try to help her. "Let me go," Jenny said. The captain held her close.

"You come below," he said.

"Let me go!" she yelled.

CHAPTER 4

TROUBLE ON THE AMAZON RIVER

The captain said nothing. Only the engine thundered as the boat made its way upriver. The captain held Jenny close. He seemed to enjoy her fright.

"We go below," he said once again.

Jenny kicked him in the leg—hard. He let go. She ran along the deck, but the crew stopped her. The captain pulled a gun from his pocket.

"We go now," he said. He was angry. His crew moved away, out of the line of fire. Jenny took a step back. The captain came towards her.

Then his foot caught in a rope. He tripped and dropped the gun. It fired as it hit the deck. The shot went into the air. The gun slid forward along the deck.

Jenny grabbed the gun, but the captain kept heading for her. Jenny didn't know if she could shoot. The captain laughed and reached out to take the gun.

Then someone pushed Jenny to the side. It was the native. He faced the captain. Now Jenny held the gun on both men. Her heart was pounding. How could I have ended up in this mess? she thought. And now what should I do?

The native did not speak. The captain's look was cold. He said a few sharp words to the native, but got no answer. Then, to Jenny's surprise, she saw that the native was telling the captain, without saying a word, to stay away from Jenny.

The captain reached out to hit the native. The native grabbed him, but the captain pulled away. They hit each other hard.

Then the native landed a great blow on the captain's chest. The captain gave a cry. He fell back over the side of the boat, into the black water.

The native rushed to the rail and looked down. He saw nothing. But on board they heard the captain cry out again. The man at the wheel didn't stop the boat or turn it around. The captain would drown for sure.

Jenny felt sick. Her hands shook, and she had

trouble holding the gun. The native came over and took it from her. Then the men in the crew made a rush at him. The native held the gun on them. There were angry words in low voices. Then the crew went back to work.

Jenny took her first easy breath in hours. She headed for the stern with the native and sat down on a box. The native sat next to her. How he had frightened her—and then he had saved her from the captain! Perhaps it was a trick. But she had let him take the gun. I'm going crazy, she thought.

The native was watching her. He still held the gun. He smiled at her, showing clean, white teeth.

"Manaus," Jenny said. "Are we going to Manaus?"

"Manaus?" the native said. "No, Manaus is downriver. This boat is headed upriver." He spoke English!

Jenny began to laugh. She laughed until the tears came. She had been running and running and running. Manaus was as far away as ever. Even more so.

"Sleep," the native said. "I'll keep watch."

Now Jenny trusted him. Sleep closed in. But she did not sleep long. She woke up to find the native still at her side. There was a small, open basket on the deck next to him. It was filled with food. The native was eating something soft and white with his fingers.

"What's your name?" Jenny asked.

"Arajo," he said.

"Ara—what?" asked Jenny.

"Arajo. That's my name."

"I'm Jenny. Jenny Parker."

Arajo reached into the basket and pulled out some food. "Would you like some?" he asked. "It's good."

Jenny was hungry, but she was afraid of the strange food. She shook her head.

Arajo put the food back into the basket. He brought out a bottle and showed it to her. "Drink this, then," he said.

"Maybe later," Jenny said.

Arajo smiled and went back to eating.

What could the food be? Jenny thought. Animal? Vegetable?

"OK, Arajo," she said, "I'll drink something to start."

He handed her the bottle. The top was off. She could see something like milk half way down. She smelled it. Soup?

Jenny closed her eyes. Here goes, she thought. She put the bottle to her mouth and took a long drink.

"Fire!" She dropped the bottle. "I'm on fire!"

The stuff seemed to burn a hole right through her. She got up and ran to the side of the boat. "Water," she yelled. "I need some water!"

But over the water she saw something else instead—something that made her heart sink. The boat was speeding right into the shore. And on the shore were some large rocks. The crew did not seem to see them. Before Jenny could call out, the crash came. She grabbed on to the rail. The boat shook and seemed to crack wide open.

Then Jenny was in the water. It closed over her, and she went under. Grabbing at a large rock, she pulled herself back up to the air. She was all right.

She looked back. The boat was sinking. It went down fast. She closed her eyes for a second and when she opened them, the boat was gone. She had to catch her breath.

Jenny climbed out of the water and on to the river bank. She looked for signs of Arajo and the crew. She could see no one—no one at all. She was alone again. Alone under a bright, Brazilian moon. Only the noises of the jungle were around her.

"Jenny!"

She turned. It was a cry. Had someone called her name? She listened. Was it Arajo? From far off she heard a laugh—or the call of a bird. She didn't know which.

CHAPTER **5**

ATTACK!

All around Jenny were strange noises. They seemed to call her name and whisper in her ears. She moved slowly along the shore line. Then an insect found her, followed by what seemed like a whole army of them. Jenny found a stick and beat them away.

"Wait, hold it. Hold it." Someone caught her arm and pulled the stick away. "Take it easy."

It was a man holding a flashlight in her eyes. He was speaking English!

"Who are you?" he asked.

"Take the light out of my eyes, please," Jenny said.

He put the light on his own face. "I'm Robert Hillson," he said. He had a kind face. Jenny knew at once that he didn't mean trouble.

"I'm Jenny Parker," she said.

"You'd better come back to the house with

me," Mr. Hillson said. "My wife and I heard your boat crash. What happened, anyway?"

"I don't really know," said Jenny, going with him. "The crew let the boat run up on the rocks. I guess they all went down with it. Or maybe they made it to shore somewhere else. I hope so. Everything's gone wrong."

"Come along, now. I must telephone the river patrol in Manaus."

Then they came to a house that looked out on the Amazon River. Myra Hillson was standing by the door waiting for them. She showed Jenny to a small bedroom and gave her some dry clothes to wear.

It was hard for Jenny to keep her eyes open. She felt so happy to be safe at last. Mrs. Hillson told her to get some sleep, and left her alone. But the jungle sounds rang in Jenny's ears. Would the noise ever stop?

"Jenny!"

There it was again! She sat up. It was like a cry for help. She listened, but it was gone. She could not get any sleep after that. Jenny got out of bed and went into the living room. Mr. and Mrs. Hillson were sitting in the soft light of an oil lamp.

"Can't sleep?" Mrs. Hillson asked.

"I thought someone called my name," said Jenny.

"That happens out here," Mr. Hillson said. "Until you get used to them, the jungle noises sound like people talking."

"I've heard the natives try to frighten people by making strange sounds," said Jenny.

"We don't worry about natives," said Mrs. Hillson, "but we *are* careful. Remember, Jenny, if anything happens here, we will all try to get away fast. We keep the car on the left side of the house. The key is in the car under the front seat."

Jenny felt a cold wind blowing right through her. "I've heard that there's trouble with the natives upriver," she said.

"Oh, that's near Tefé, about 10 miles away," said Mr. Hillson. "There's a little trouble up there, now and then. The soldiers are there now." Mr. Hillson smiled. "Don't worry. That's 10 miles away."

"Let's talk about other things," said Mrs. Hillson. "Jenny, do you want to tell us what you were doing on the boat?"

"I've asked myself the same question. I guess

I was going to Manaus the wrong way," said Jenny.

Both Hillsons laughed. "Could you explain that?" Mrs. Hillson asked.

Jenny said, "I've been trying to get to Manaus, but I haven't been very lucky so far."

"Why Manaus?" asked Mrs. Hillson.

"To catch a plane to Rio," answered Jenny. "I'm trying to get back to Boston."

"Oh, dear," said Mrs. Hillson. "I guess you lost everything on the boat."

Jenny didn't want to explain more than necessary. "That's right," she said.

"Well," said Mrs. Hillson, "you can be sure that we'll help you. We'll see that you get to Manaus."

Jenny smiled. Soon she would be on her way.

"But now you're going to eat," said Mrs. Hillson. "And then you must get some sleep."

She woke up with a start. Had someone called her? Or was it the jungle noises again? Jenny had no idea what time it was. It was black outside the bedroom. She heard one long, low cry—a human cry. No animal can sound like that, she thought.

Jenny climbed out of bed. She got dressed. She was worried, but she couldn't explain why. She went out into the living room. Mr. and Mrs. Hillson had gone to bed. It was hot. Jenny went outside the house to cool off.

There was a long, rolling sound far away. Thunder. It was going to rain.

Suddenly she heard a scream. It came from inside the house. She ran to a window and looked in. It was the Hillson's bedroom—and it was on fire! She could see human shapes in the light of the fire. Natives!

The Hillsons lay across the bed. She could see blood where the arrows had hit. Dead! The Hillsons were *dead*. Jenny knew they were dead. There was nothing she could do to help them now. But she knew that she had to get away fast. If the natives caught her she thought they would kill her, too!

She raced to the car and climbed in. She found the key, but the engine wouldn't start. Then she spotted a native running towards the car. Thunder crashed. Rain fell in great sheets.

She tried to start the car again. This time it started. Suddenly the native was right in front of her. She started the car moving—fast. At the

last second, the man jumped out of the way.

Jenny turned into the road. "Manaus," she said to herself. "I must get to Manaus, no matter what!"

The rain didn't let up. The road was washed out in spots. Once or twice the car hit deep potholes in the road. She thought she would have to stop.

Then the car lights picked out something

strange ahead. It stood in the road and looked at her with shining eyes.

"What is it?" she asked. Her heart was beating fast. Was it man or animal? It was covered with hair and had a long nose—a big anteater! It stood up on its hind legs in front of the car without moving.

Jenny didn't want to hit it. She made a sharp

turn to the right. The car hit a pothole and went out of control.

The car began sliding down the bank to the river. It rolled over twice and came to a dead stop, its wheels covered by water.

CHAPTER **6**

SPILLED VEGETABLES

"Senhorita." A man's voice was calling her. Jenny heard a tap-tap-tap on the car window.

"Senhorita."

Jenny was almost folded in two on the car seat. She was awake now—fully awake. Her body was stiff and sore, but she knew nothing was broken. She blinked at the light. It was morning now.

"Senhorita." The car door was torn open. A hand reached in and took hold of her arm.

"Please. Take it easy!" Jenny said.

A soldier with a gun held on to her arm. "You hurt?" he asked.

"I don't think so," Jenny said.

"Then we go," the soldier said. He helped her to get out of the car. Slowly they climbed up the bank to the road, where there was a lorry waiting.

The soldier helped Jenny get in beside him. He took the wheel. Jenny knew she was OK now. Luck was with her at last, she thought.

"Where are you going?" Jenny asked the soldier. "Manaus? Can you take me to Manaus?" He did not answer. He looked straight ahead. No luck after all.

They drove a few miles and stopped. Jenny took a deep breath. There was a camp beside the road with five or six tents in it.

"What's this?" she asked the soldier.

"Come," he said.

She got out of the lorry and followed him. A few soldiers stood around and watched them.

"Chief here," he said, showing her a tent. "Go into this tent."

"Why?" asked Jenny. "Tell me who you are. Who is this chief?" But he pushed her into the tent. The tent was empty except for a bed, some chairs, and a table. There was no chief, whoever he was.

She waited for a few seconds without moving, remembering the boat captain. But the soldier didn't come into the tent.

She asked herself what she was supposed to do now.

She heard voices and looked outside. Some soldiers were keeping an eye on the tent. What did they want of her? She had questions to ask but no one to answer them.

She waited for a while, but time moved slowly. Then Jenny got up and checked outside the tent again. To her surprise, the soldiers were gone. She couldn't believe it. "They must think I'll really wait for their chief," she said out loud. "But I won't."

She slipped out of the tent. They might be eating, she thought. She raced for the road.

I went through the same thing yesterday, she thought. Only then I was running away from Arajo. Poor Arajo, I'll never forget him. He scared me half to death, but he was really a friend after all. I hope he's OK. I'd like to see him again.

Jenny had gone about a mile when she saw a few chickens. Then some children crossed the road and waved at her. At last, she thought. I'll be seeing people again. Crowds of people. Hundreds of people.

She came to a clearing right near the river. In it was an outside market, full of people—just

what she wanted. And there was food. The food smelled good.

She stopped. The food smelled good, all right —but she had no money to buy it! And she was in a market far away from Manaus and Rio. It was a market along the Amazon River at the end of the world.

"Senhorita!" She heard someone yell from across the market.

Jenny turned and looked. Soldiers again! They had found her. They began running around the market trying to get to her. She ran. She didn't want to spend the rest of her life in jail. For doing what? For being scared to death by a giant anteater? They were after her. But why? No one would explain. She wasn't waiting to find out. She raced on.

Jenny didn't look where she was going. She smashed into a vegetable stand. Vegetables spilled to the ground.

She heard an angry cry, but she kept running. I'll pay them back later, she thought to herself. I really will. If only I can get away from here. If only I can escape.

An angry crowd circled her. She was trapped. Hands reached out and pulled her down. Then she heard the voice.

The words were in Portuguese, but she knew the voice. She'd know that voice anywhere. Slowly she looked up.

The crowd looked down at her, but Jenny saw only one face.

"You!" she whispered.

CHAPTER 7
BLOOD IS DRAWN

Strong arms pulled Jenny up. Cliff Bodine stared at her with a look of anger and surprise. Then, without saying a word, he led her out of the market to a waiting lorry.

He sat at the wheel of the lorry, next to her, but he didn't say a word. He started the engine and moved out. Behind them was a second lorry—full of soldiers.

When they were on the main road, Cliff spoke at last.

"Jenny, what in the world are you doing here, with half the market pulled down around you?" He was upset. Jenny felt sick. She just sat there, looking at the road ahead. She was seated next to the man she had come so many miles to marry. But there was one thing wrong —one *big* thing wrong. He couldn't care less. He was not the Cliff she had loved in Boston.

"Do you know the danger you've walked in-to? The trouble you've caused me?" Cliff was asking. "How can I explain it to these people?"

Jenny turned to Cliff, angry. "You *do* remember me, don't you? Jenny Parker? We met in Boston. Remember?" She stopped and waited. She really tried to stay calm. But Cliff was acting so strangely that he made Jenny say things she didn't want to say—ever.

Jenny went on. "Once someone asked me to marry him. As I remember it, his name was Cliff Bodine."

Cliff drove on, his eyes on the road. Then he turned to her. "As I remember it, you weren't too sure."

Jenny said, "As I remember it, the last words I said to you were 'I love you.' "

Cliff's eyes were back on the road. "The last word you said to me was 'Goodbye.' "

"I wrote to you," said Jenny. "I wrote that I was coming to Brazil. I said I would marry you. Are you telling me you never saw that letter? Is that why you didn't meet me? Is that why no one at your house knew who I was? I don't believe that's the truth, Cliff."

Cliff stopped the lorry at the camp. He

jumped out and went into the chief's tent, without waiting for Jenny.

Jenny sat still. The second lorry came to a stop. The soldiers got out but didn't look at her. It was as if she was not there.

She jumped out of the lorry and went into the tent. Cliff was sitting at the table, reading some papers.

"So you're the chief," Jenny said. "What *are* you doing here? I thought you were a farmer. A pioneer. That's just another lie. One of many."

"Sit down," Cliff said, pointing to a chair.

She didn't sit down.

Cliff put down his papers. "Jenny, what's all this about lies? There's big native trouble here right now. When there's trouble with the Tupi-Guarani people, the soldiers ask for my help. I *am* a farmer, and I can speak Tupi-Guarani. When the soldiers came for me, I had to leave Bodine Ranch right away. I came up here with them. That's why I couldn't meet you."

"OK," said Jenny. "I understand what you're doing here, now, this minute. But I wish you had explained *everything* about yourself in Boston. You could have saved me a long, hard trip."

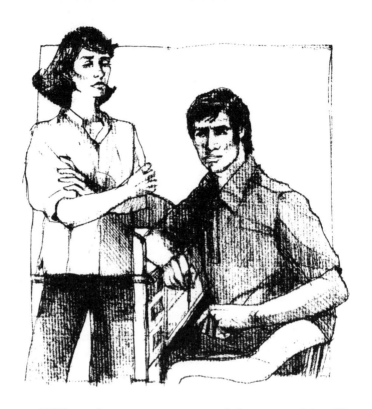

"What do you mean, explain everything?" asked Cliff. "I think it's your turn to do some explaining. How did you get all the way out here? How did you find me?"

"Figure it out for yourself," said Jenny. She walked out of the tent.

Jenny crossed the road and went to the river bank. She looked down at the Amazon. The water was rushing by.

I'll get to Manaus if I have to swim there, she thought. I never want to see that man again as long as I live. But she knew she was saying words with no meaning.

"Senhorita."

One of the soldiers stood on the road. "Come," he said.

Jenny looked up at him. She felt very tired. All her fight was gone—at least for the moment. "OK, I'm coming," she said. She climbed slowly up the river bank and went back to the tent with the soldier. Cliff was nowhere in sight.

"Where is the chief?" Jenny asked.

"Tupi-Guarani," the soldier said, and left her alone in the tent. She sat down and took a deep breath.

Stop fooling yourself, Jenny Parker, she thought to herself. You still love him. You still love Cliff Bodine, even if he's married. Even if he's acting strangely. Even if his wife is about to have a baby.

Then it came to her. "Tupi-Guarani," the soldier had said. The natives must be out there somewhere, and Cliff had gone to them. Did he know about the Hillsons? Did he know what the Tupi-Guarani had done?

Her heart beat fast. She had to see Cliff, to tell him before it was too late. Jenny ran out of the tent and looked around. The camp was empty.

Then, in a jungle clearing nearby, she saw soldiers. Jenny began to run. As she came close, she saw that Cliff was with them. He saw her at the same time.

"Get back," he called. "Get out of here! Do you want to get killed?"

She started to speak. "Cliff, I must talk to you."

"I said go back. Get out of here. Get away!" His voice was loud and angry.

Jenny turned back. Suddenly she felt as if her arm was burning. She touched the spot. It was wet with her own blood.

CHAPTER 8
JUNGLE JENNY

"Get down!" Cliff raced to Jenny's side. He pulled her to the ground. Arrows were flying over their heads. Then he saw the blood on her arm. His face grew white. "You're hit!" he said. "But it doesn't look too bad. Are you OK?"

Jenny nodded.

"Keep low and follow me," he said.

Slowly they made their way back to camp. As they walked, they heard the sound of the soldiers' guns firing. Once inside the tent, Cliff cleaned the blood off her arm. Then he put a clean rag around the cut. He didn't speak. Jenny didn't say a word either. Yet it seemed to Jenny as if a hundred words passed between them.

Then Cliff looked at her. "We have a lot to say to one another," he said at last.

Jenny took a deep breath. "Yes, we do," she said.

"But not here," he said. "At least not right now. I must get back. The natives are ready to talk peace. At least they were until you showed up. Will you agree to stay right here until I come back? I mean it, Jenny, don't move."

"Cliff, I must talk to you. About the Hillsons," Jenny said.

Cliff put his hand to her mouth. "Not another word, Jenny. Not now. I know about the Hillsons. Now please stay here. I'll be back. That's a promise."

He turned and left the tent. Jenny went to the opening. She saw him move slowly out of the camp toward the clearing in the jungle.

Jenny stepped outside the tent. Everything seemed still now. The soldiers waited. And in the jungle, the Tupi-Guarani people were waiting, too. For what?

Hours seemed to go by. The sun was high and hot. The screaming of birds and monkeys, all the jungle sounds, seemed to go on and on. Jenny thought about Maria and the baby. She could think clearly now. For the first time since she came to Brazil, she felt easy. She wasn't afraid. She felt strong again—at peace with herself. And she knew she loved Cliff more than ever before. She *would* tell him. Then she would return to Boston. And she would never see him again. That was the way it had to be. Her mind was made up.

Suddenly a native stepped out of the jungle. He was tall, and he moved in a slow, easy way.

Jenny gasped. Arajo! Arajo wasn't dead! Her heart stopped for a second. She wanted to shout hello.

Arajo turned and saw her at the tent. They stared at one another without speaking. Then Arajo raised his hand in greeting.

"Jenny Parker," he called. "You can come out here, Jenny Parker. It is safe now."

Jenny walked up to him and held out her hand. Arajo smiled and took her hand in his. Then Cliff Bodine came out of the trees.

Cliff couldn't say a word. He looked first at Jenny and then at Arajo, his mouth open.

"I think I've been in the jungle too long," he said with great surprise. "The next thing you're going to say is that you're old friends. Right, Jenny?"

"Right," said Jenny. "Arajo, *you* tell him." The two men walked away.

It took hours, it seemed. Hours for Arajo, chief of the Tupi-Guarani people, and Cliff Bodine, leader of the pioneer farmers, to talk peace.

Then the two men smiled and shook hands. Arajo came over to Jenny, inside the tent, and took her hand in his. Their eyes met. "My people will stay at peace now," he said to her. "And you, Jenny Parker. My people watched you in

the jungle. At first we wanted to kill you. But you have shown us something my people understand. You are brave in great trouble."

Cliff put his arm around Jenny. "Arajo told me some parts of your story, Jenny. He stayed with you almost all the way even when you didn't know it. And on the river boat, he liked your spirit. He says you are clever and quick—like a bird of the jungle. He calls you Jungle Jenny now."

Jenny's eyes opened wide. "He does?" she said.

Arajo smiled. Then he left the tent. Jenny was alone with Cliff. The sun had gone down. He lit an oil lamp. It threw off a soft light.

"Shall we begin at the beginning?" Cliff asked.

"From the beginning in Boston or the beginning in Brazil?" Jenny answered.

"From the beginning—well, it doesn't really matter. I sent a message for you to the airport in Manaus. I said to wait in Manaus until I came for you."

"There was no message for me," said Jenny. "I asked all around the airport. I don't think you left a message for me, Cliff. Face it, I don't think you wanted me to come to Brazil. I think I was your little affair in Boston, that's all."

Cliff looked angry.

"What do you mean, little affair? Jenny, you've said something about lies, too. What *are* you talking about?"

Jenny stared at Cliff. "There's nothing you want to explain?"

"Explain? No, it's your turn, Jenny. You've been acting strangely. What's on your mind?"

Jenny laughed. "Me, acting strangely? They are very funny words coming from you. You're the one who is strange. What do you plan to do with me? Marry me too? Isn't *that* just a bit strange? Maybe you *have* been in the jungle too long."

"Marry you too?" Cliff asked. "What are you talking about?"

"How can you explain Maria away?"

Cliff looked as if he didn't know what she was saying. "Maria?"

"Maria? With black hair? On Bodine Ranch? You never heard of the Maria who's going to have your baby?"

"Maria? You mean Ricardo's wife? She's going to have *my* baby? Well, that's the first I've heard of it."

Jenny bit her lip. "Who's Ricardo?"

"He helps me run Bodine Ranch." Then Cliff looked at her and began to laugh. "You don't mean—dear Jenny," Cliff said. "You went through all this because you thought Maria and I—"

Jenny smiled a weak smile. "I couldn't help but think so. I couldn't talk to the people at your house. No one spoke English. I asked Maria where her husband was. She answered 'Senhor Bodine away.' Maybe she really didn't know what I had asked. But that did it anyway. I said, Jenny, get out of here. Get back to Boston—fast!"

"Well, you can stop running now," Cliff said.

"Cliff, you once said that people need to be strong to live in the jungle. I've been in the jungle for many hours and I'm still alive."

Cliff took her hand. "You're very much alive, Jenny. I'm proud of you. And I want to spend my life with you. You're a fine pioneer. But you *need* to learn to speak Portuguese!"

"Oh, I'll learn Portuguese all right," Jenny

said. "But live here a lifetime—" She smiled. "That's a long while."

Cliff drew her to him. "Come on, now, Jungle Jenny," he said. "You've passed all your tests. And I've passed all mine."

They looked deeply into each other's eyes. Then they walked off to the lorry, their arms around each other.